PLUGGED IN

Electric Riddles

by Scott K. Peterson
pictures by Susan Slattery Burke

Lerner Publications Company
Minneapolis

To all the past and present members of the band Flashback: Denny, Dale, Al, John, Chris, Tom, Gary, Lee, Jay, and myself. Thanks for all the memories. —S.K.P.

To Nick, for all his love and support —S.S.B.

This book is available in two editions:
Library binding by Lerner Publications Company
Soft cover by First Avenue Editions
241 First Avenue North
Minneapolis, MN 55401

Library of Congress Cataloging-in-Publication Data

Peterson, Scott K.
  Plugged in : electric riddles / by Scott K. Peterson ; pictures
by Susan Slattery Burke.
     p.   cm. — (You must be joking!)
  ISBN 0-8225-2344-2 (lib. bdg.) ISBN 0-8225-9700-4 (pbk.)
  1. Riddles, Juvenile. 2. Electric apparatus and appliances—
Juvenile humor. [1. Riddles. 2. Jokes. 3. Electric apparatus and
appliances—Wit and humor.] I. Burke, Susan Slattery, ill. II. Title.
III. Series.
PN6371.5.P474 1995
818'.5402—dc20   94-24871

Manufactured in the United States of America

1 2 3 4 5 6 – I/JR – 00 99 98 97 96 95

Q: What do lamps wear on sunny days?

A: Their shades.

Q: What would you call a telephone with feet?

A: A walkie-talkie.

Q: Why did the telephone call a cab?

A: Because it had to travel long-distance.

Q: How does a radio count to ten?

A: 1, 2, 3, 4, 5, 6, 7, 8, 9, antenna.

Q: How did the flies
get inside the TV set?

A: There was a hole
in its screen.

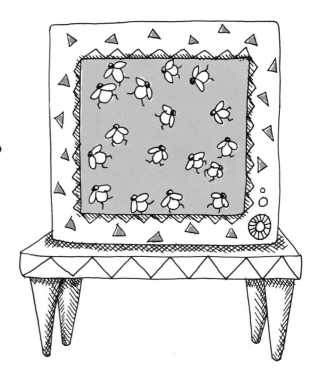

Q: What do you call a 36-inch lightbulb?
A: A yard light.

Q: What does a lightbulb do with a punching bag?
A: It likes to socket.

Q: Why don't flashlights buy flowers?
A: Because they have their own bulbs.

Q: Why didn't the lightbulb go to college?
A: Because it wasn't very bright.

Q: Why don't doorbells go to college?
A: Because they're dingdongs.

Q: What's a good name for a light?
A: Spot.

Q: What's a vacuum cleaner's favorite sport?
A: Rugby.

Q: Why did the vacuum cleaner learn
self-defense?
A: It was tired of being pushed around.

Q: What's a vacuum cleaner's favorite candy?
A: A sucker.

Q: What's an X-ray machine's favorite food?
A: Ribs.

Q: What's a lightbulb's favorite food?
A: Lamp chops.

Q: What do lighthouses eat for breakfast?
A: Beacon and eggs.

Q: Why did the army private buy a popcorn popper?
A: Because she wanted to make a kernel someday.

Q: How do you ask a lightbulb if something is wrong?

A: "Watts the matter?"

Q: How do you keep two electric frying pans from arguing with each other?

A: Tell them to simmer down.

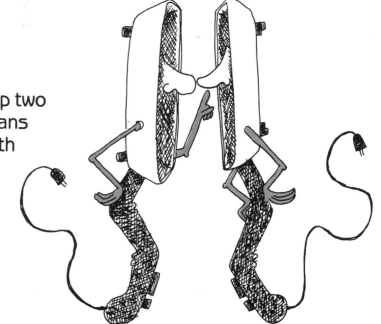

Q: What do you do if your coffeemaker is depressed?
A. Try to perk it up.

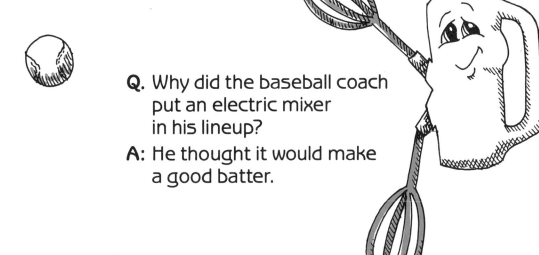

Q. Why did the baseball coach
put an electric mixer
in his lineup?
A: He thought it would make
a good batter.

Q: Why did the astronaut take his furnace to the moon?

A: He wanted to make a space heater.

Q: Why did the man drive in the lightning storm?

A: Because his car needed shocks.

Q: Why didn't the tightrope walker take any money out of the cash machine?

A: He needed to keep his balance.

Q: Why can't ceiling fans stay at one job for very long?

A: Because they have such a big turnaround.

Q: Why did the woman buy track shoes for her refrigerator?

A: Because it was always running.

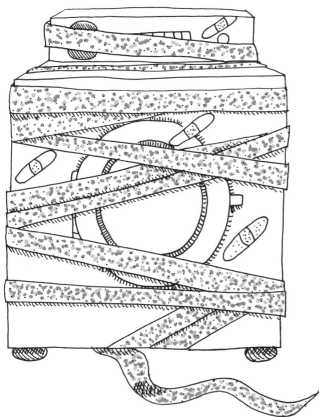

Q: Why was the clothes dryer bandaged up?

A: It took a bad tumble.

Q: Why was the record player pulled over on the highway?

A: It kept changing speeds.

Q: Why did the fish jump out of the tanning bed?

A: It didn't want to get fried.

Q: Why did the man replace his grandfather clock with a new electric clock?

A: Because it was an old timer.

Q: Why is it hard to buy gloves for clocks?

A: Because they have different-sized hands.

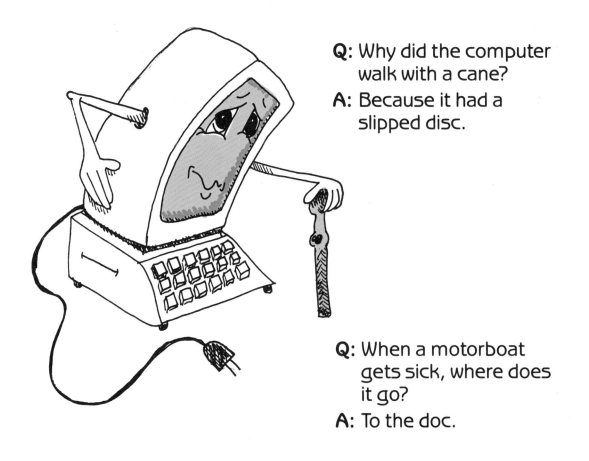

Q: Why did the computer walk with a cane?

A: Because it had a slipped disc.

Q: When a motorboat gets sick, where does it go?

A: To the doc.

Q: Why did the TV set start shaving?

A: Because its picture was getting fuzzy.

Q: Why is it so easy to talk to a pencil sharpener?

A: Because they get right to the point.

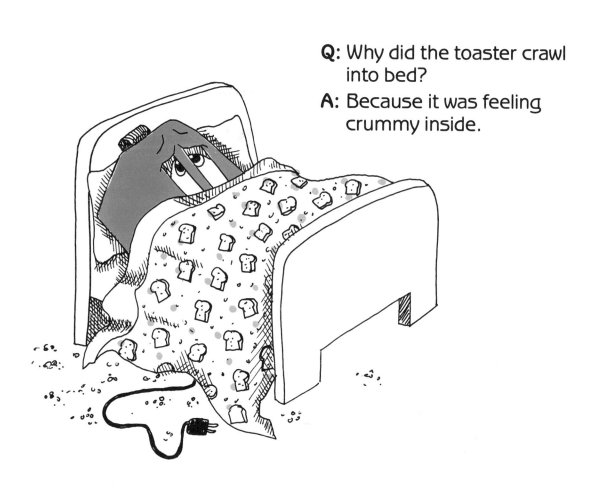

Q: Why did the toaster crawl into bed?

A: Because it was feeling crummy inside.

Q: Why was the iron in such a big hurry?
A: It was pressed for time.

Q: How do cameras take pictures?
A: In a flash.

Q: Why do blenders go to so many parties?
A: Because they mix so well with everyone.

Q: Why did the two magnets fall in love?
A: Because they were attracted to each other.

Q: What happened after the two TV sets got married?
A. They had a nice reception.

Q: Why are batteries always confused?

A: Because they're both negative and positive about everything.

Q: How do batteries buy things?

A: With their charges.

Q: How can you tell when a thermostat is sick?

A: It has a high temperature.

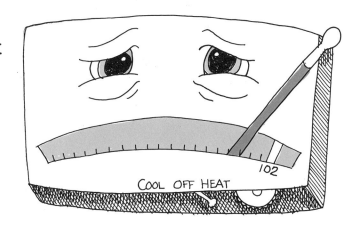

COOL OFF HEAT

102

Q: How do electric skillets keep warm at night?

A: They keep their covers on.

Q: Why was the electric razor so nervous?

A: It had a close shave.

Q: How do deep-sea divers fix the picture on their TV sets?

A: They use their tunas.

Q: How can you tell when deep freezers are asleep?

A: When their lids are closed.

Q: Why did the electric saw jump into the freezer?

A: It wanted to make some cold cuts.

Q: Why did the adding machine go on a diet?

A: It wanted a better figure.

Q: Why did the air conditioner wear sunglasses?

A: Because it wanted to be cooler.

Q: Why was the garage door opener hitchhiking?

A: Because it needed a lift.

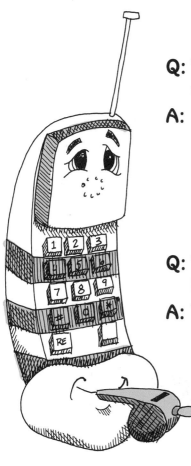

Q: Why does a telephone make a good referee?

A: Because it makes good calls.

Q: What's a coffeemaker's favorite baseball team?

A: The Brewers.

Q: What's a good name for an electric lawn mower?
A: Moe.

Q: Why didn't the lightbulb light up in the river?

A: There wasn't enough current.

Q: How did the lightning bolt become president?

A: It had the most volts.

Q: What do pigs want to be when they grow up?

A: Ham radio operators.

Q: What do you say to your headlights on a dark country road?

A: "Hi beams!"

Q: What kind of sound does a golf cart make?
A: Putt putt putt.

Q: Why don't you ever see radios reading books?

A: They're always too busy playing.

Q: Why shouldn't you take advice from furnaces?

A: Because they just blow hot air.

Q: Why don't plumbers like coffeemakers?

A: They don't like to see all those drips.

Q: How can you tell when a sewing machine is laughing?

A: Because it's in stitches.

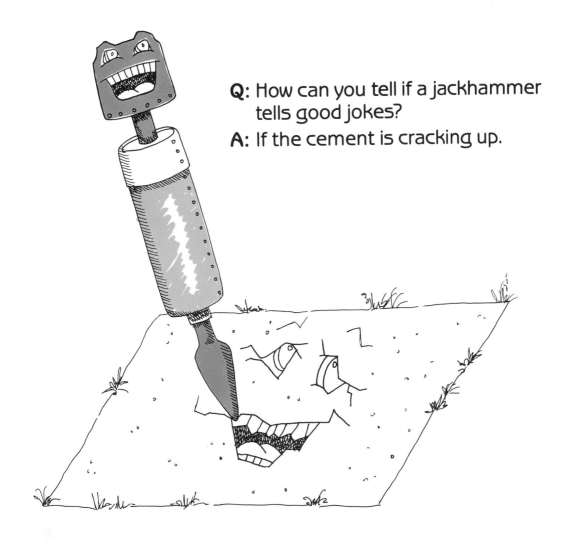

Q: How can you tell if a jackhammer tells good jokes?

A: If the cement is cracking up.

ABOUT THE AUTHOR

Scott K. Peterson has always been able to make somebody laugh about something, as anyone who knows him will tell you. A graduate of Coon Rapids High School, he has lived in Minnesota all of his life. While he's not working or thinking up jokes, Scott enjoys fishing, playing the drums, cartooning, and spending time with his wife and three children.

ABOUT THE ARTIST

Susan Slattery Burke loves to illustrate fun-loving characters, especially animals. To her, each of her characters has a personality all its own. She is most satisfied when the characters come to life for the reader as well. Susan lives in Minnetonka, Minnesota, with her husband, two daughters, and their dog and cat. Susan enjoys sculpting, reading, traveling, illustrating, and chasing her children around.

You Must Be Joking books

Alphabatty
Riddles from A to Z

Class Act
Riddles for School

Help Wanted
Riddles about Jobs

Here's to Ewe
Riddles about Sheep

Hide and Shriek
Riddles about Ghosts
and Goblins

Ho Ho Ho!
Riddles about
Santa Claus

Home on the Range
Ranch-Style Riddles

Hoop-La
Riddles about Basketball

I Toad You So
Riddles about Frogs and Toads

Off Base
Riddles about Baseball

On with the Show
Show Me Riddles

Out on a Limb
Riddles about Trees
and Plants

Out to Dry
Riddles about Deserts

Playing Possum
Riddles about Kangaroos,
Koalas, and Other Marsupials

Plugged In
Electric Riddles

Summit Up
Riddles about Mountains

Take a Hike
Riddles about Football

That's for Shore
Riddles from the Beach

Weather or Not
Riddles for Rain and Shine

What's Gnu?
Riddles from the Zoo

Wing It!
Riddles about Birds